EASY GUITAR WITH NOTES & TAB

Top Hits of 2017

8 BELIEVER
Imagine Dragons

12 BODY LIKE A BACK ROAD
Sam Hunt

16 BROKEN HALOS
Chris Stapleton

3 CHAINED TO THE RHYTHM
Katy Perry

20 CITY OF STARS
Ryan Gosling & Emma Stone

24 DESPACITO
Luis Fonsi & Daddy Yankee featuring Justin Bieber

31 HUMAN
Rag'n'Bone Man

36 LOOK WHAT YOU MADE ME DO
Taylor Swift

40 SHAPE OF YOU
Ed Sheeran

45 SIGN OF THE TIMES
Harry Styles

50 SLOW HANDS
Niall Horan

58 THAT'S WHAT I LIKE
Bruno Mars

54 THERE'S NOTHING HOLDIN' ME BACK
Shawn Mendes

ISBN 978-1-5400-0302-7

HAL•LEONARD®

7777 W. BLUEMOUND RD. P.O. BOX 13819 MILWAUKEE, WI 53213

Visit Hal Leonard Online at
www.halleonard.com

STRUM AND PICK PATTERNS

This chart contains the suggested strum and pick patterns that are referred to by number at the beginning of each song in this book. The symbols ⊓ and ∨ in the strum patterns refer to down and up strokes, respectively. The letters in the pick patterns indicate which right-hand fingers play which strings.

p = thumb
i = index finger
m = middle finger
a = ring finger

For example; Pick Pattern 2
is played: thumb - index - middle - ring

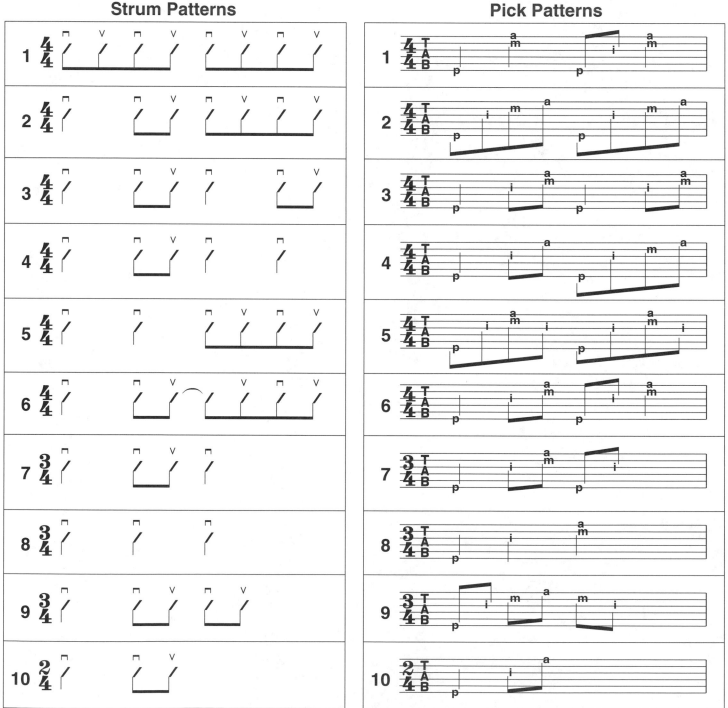

Chained to the Rhythm

Words and Music by Katy Perry, Max Martin, Sia Furler, Ali Payami and Skip Marley

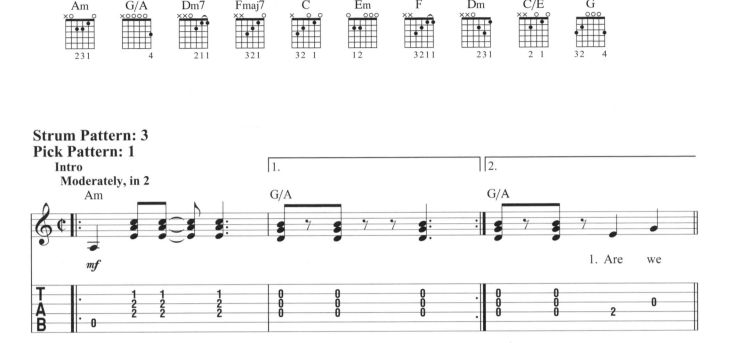

Strum Pattern: 3
Pick Pattern: 1

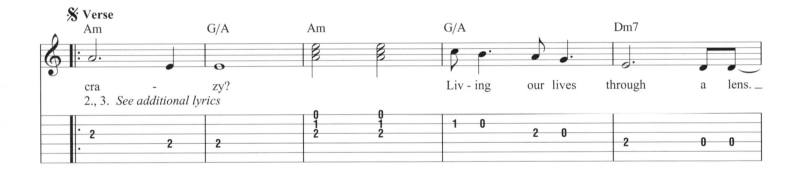

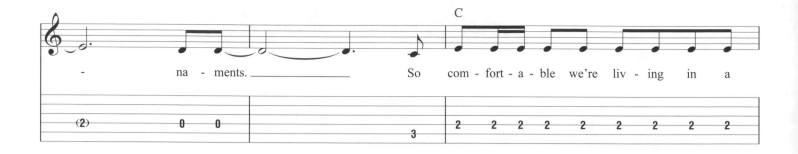

-na - ments. _____ So com - fort - a - ble we're liv - ing in a

bub - ble, bub - ble. So com - fort - a - ble we can - not see the trou - ble, trou - ble. 2. Aren't you

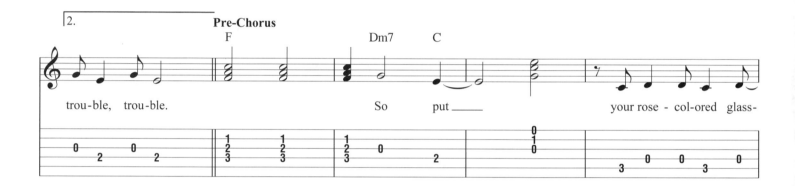

trou - ble, trou - ble. So put _____ your rose - col - ored glass-

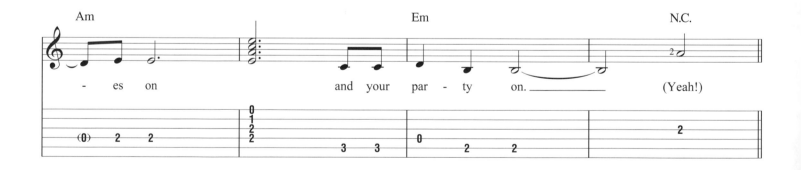

-es on and your par - ty on. _____ (Yeah!)

Turn it up, it's your fa - v'rite song, dance, dance, dance to the dis - tor - tion. _____

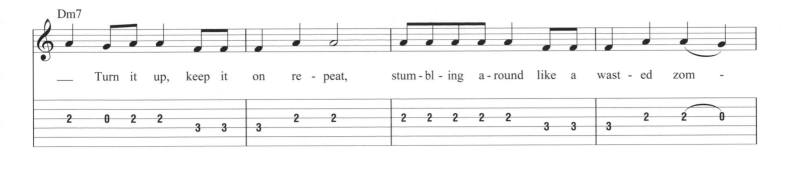

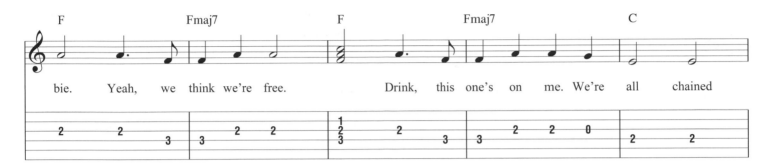

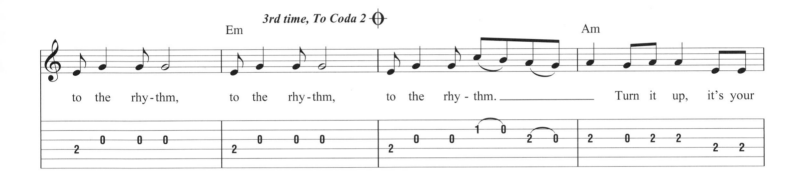

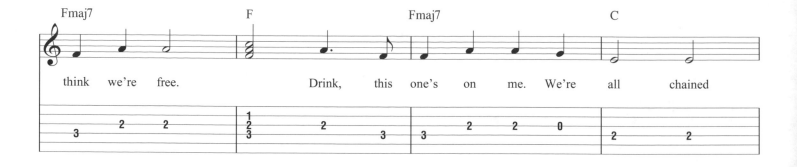

think we're free. Drink, this one's on me. We're all chained

D.S. al Coda 1
(take 2nd ending)

To Coda 1

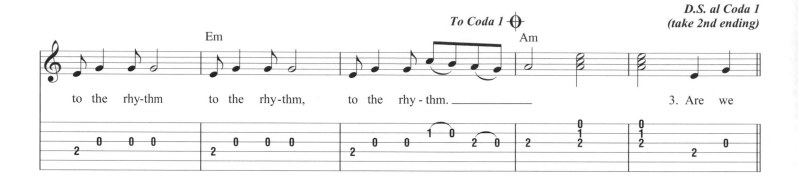

to the rhy-thm to the rhy-thm, to the rhy-thm. _____ 3. Are we

Coda 1

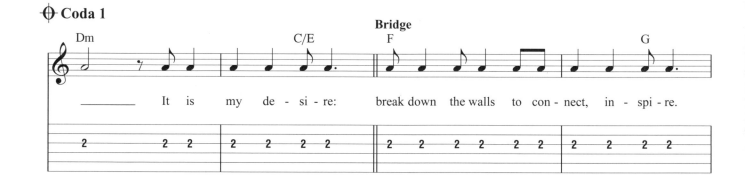

_____ It is my de-si-re: break down the walls to con-nect, in-spi-re.

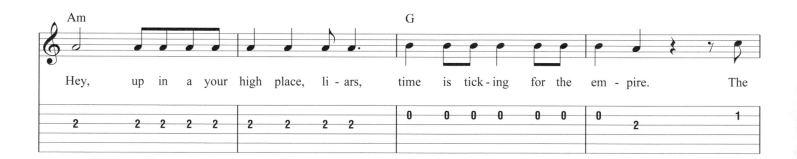

Hey, up in a your high place, li-ars, time is tick-ing for the em-pire. The

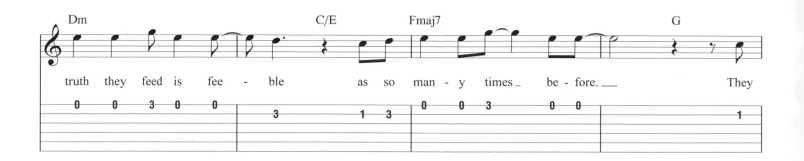

truth they feed is fee-ble as so man-y times_ be-fore.__ They

Believer

Words and Music by Dan Reynolds, Wayne Sermon, Ben McKee, Daniel Platzman,
Justin Trantor, Mattias Larsson and Robin Fredricksson

sail,   I'm   the   mas-ter   of   my   sea,   oh,   ooh, _____   the   mas-ter   of   my   sea,   oh,   ooh. _____
heard   has   turned   your   spir-it   to   a   dove,   oh,   ooh, _____   your   spir-it   up   a-bove,   oh,   ooh. _____

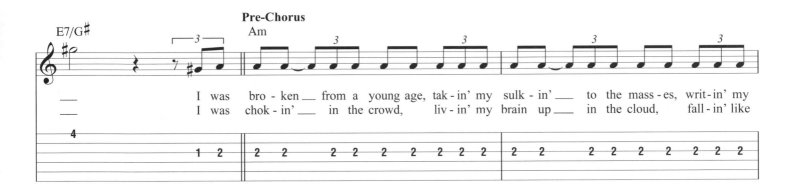

Pre-Chorus

_____   I   was   bro-ken _____   from   a   young   age,   tak-in'   my   sulk-in' _____   to   the   mass-es,   writ-in'   my
_____   I   was   chok-in' _____   in   the   crowd,   liv-in'   my   brain   up _____   in   the   cloud,   fall-in'   like

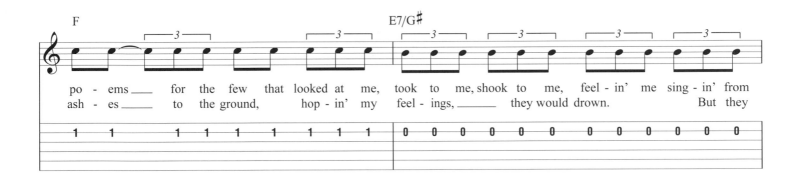

po-ems _____   for   the   few   that   looked   at   me,   took   to   me, shook   to   me,   feel-in'   me   sing-in'   from
ash-es _____   to   the   ground,   hop-in'   my   feel-ings, _____   they   would   drown.   But   they

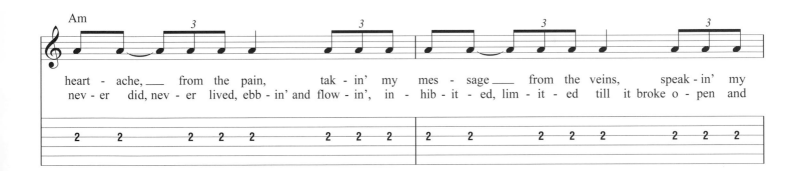

heart-ache, _____   from   the   pain,   tak-in'   my   mes-sage _____   from   the   veins,   speak-in'   my
nev-er   did, nev-er   lived,   ebb-in'   and   flow-in',   in-hib-it-ed,   lim-it-ed   till   it   broke   o-pen   and

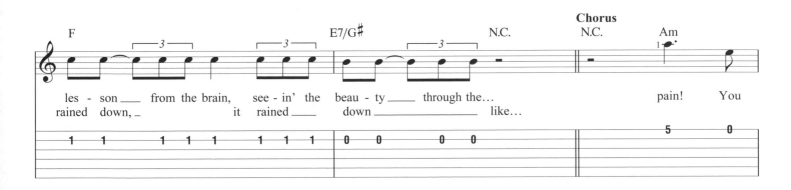

Chorus

les-son _____   from   the   brain,   see-in'   the   beau-ty _____   through   the...   pain!   You
rained   down, _   it   rained _____   down _____   like...

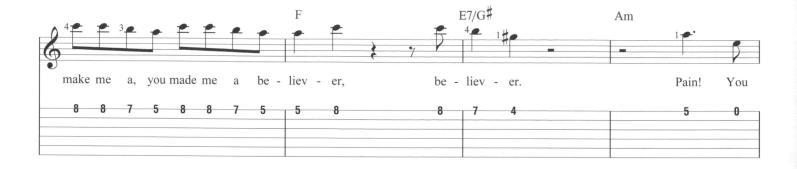

make me a, you made me a be - liev - er, be - liev - er. Pain! You

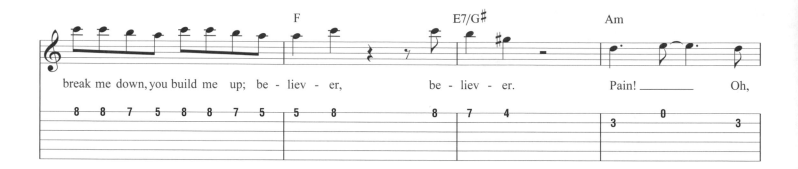

break me down, you build me up; be - liev - er, be - liev - er. Pain! _____ Oh,

let the bul - lets fly, oh, let them rain. _____ My life, my love, my drive, they came from...

1.

pain! You made me a, you made me a be - liev - er, be - liev - er.

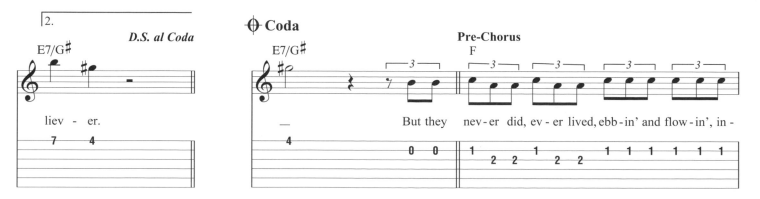

2.

D.S. al Coda

Coda

Pre-Chorus

liev - er.

But they nev - er did, ev - er lived, ebb - in' and flow - in', in -

hib-it-ed, lim-it-ed, till it broke o-pen and rained down, it rained down_ like... pain! You

made me a, you made me a be-liev-er, be-liev-er. Pain! You

break me down, you build me up; be-liev-er, be-liev-er. Pain!_____ Oh,

let the bul-lets fly, oh, let them rain._____ My life, my love, my drive, they came from...

pain! You made me a, you made me a be-liev-er, be-liev-er.

Additional Lyrics

4. Last things last: By the grace of the fire and the flames,
   You're the face of the future, the blood in my veins, oh, ooh,
   The blood in my veins, oh, ooh.

Body Like a Back Road

Words and Music by Sam Hunt, Josh Osborne, Shane McAnally and Zach Crowell

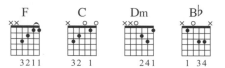

Strum Pattern: 3
Pick Pattern: 3

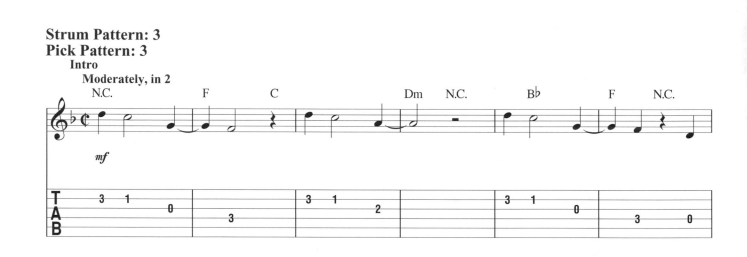

1. Got a girl from the south side,
2., 3. *See additional lyrics*

*Play F, 2nd & 3rd times.

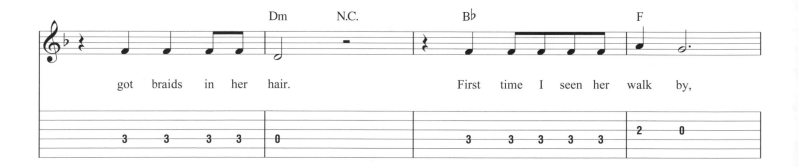

got braids in her hair.   First time I seen her walk by,

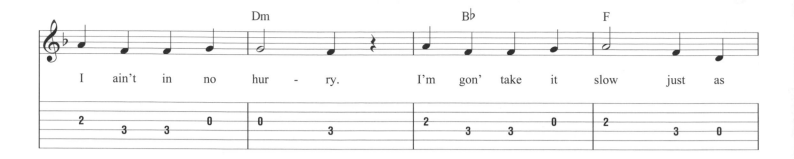

I ain't in no hur- ry. I'm gon' take it slow just as

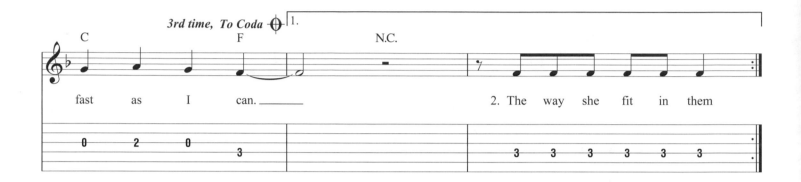

fast as I can. _____ 2. The way she fit in them

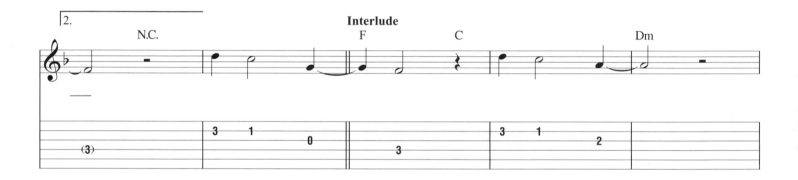

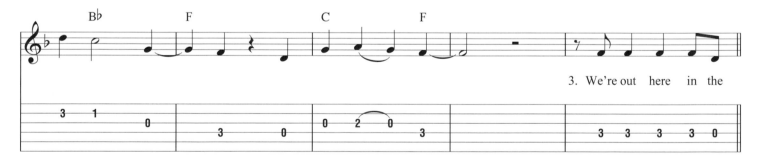

3. We're out here in the

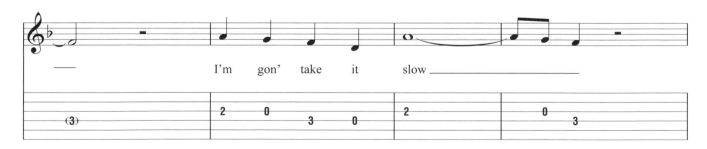

I'm gon' take it slow _____

Outro

just as fast as I can. _____

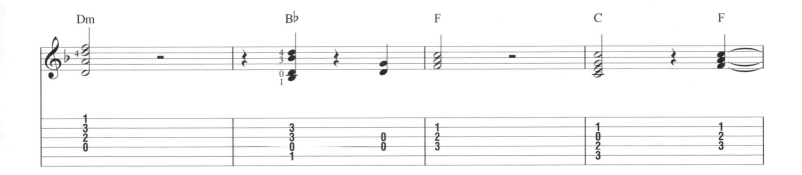

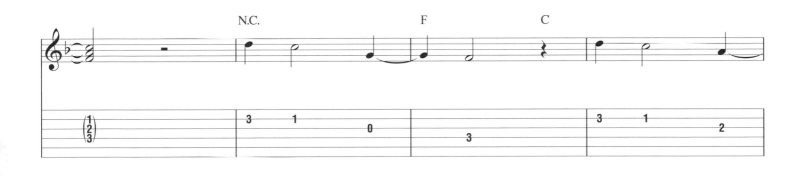

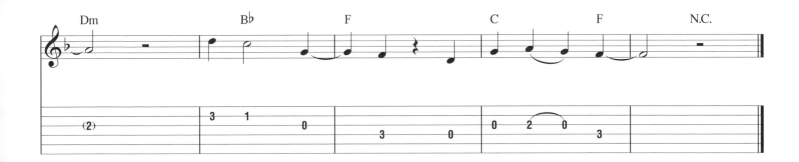

Additional Lyrics

2. The way she fit in them blue jeans, she don't need no belt.
   But I can turn 'em inside out; I don't need no help.
   Got hips like honey, so thick and so sweet.
   There ain't no curves like hers on them downtown streets.

3. We're out here in the boondocks with the breeze and the birds,
   Tangled up in the tall grass with my lips on hers.
   On the highway to heaven, headed south of her smile.
   Get there when we get there, every inch is a mile.

Broken Halos

Words and Music by Chris Stapleton and Mike Henderson

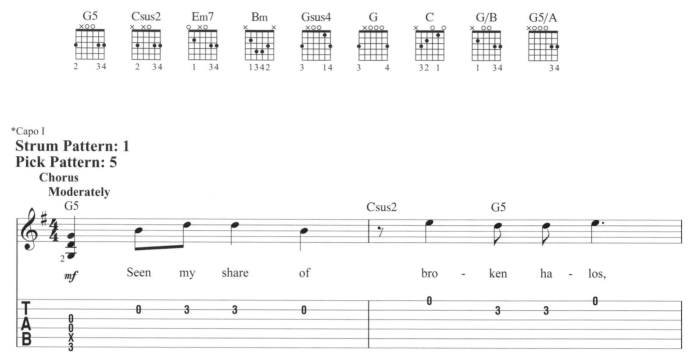

*Capo I

Strum Pattern: 1
Pick Pattern: 5

Chorus
Moderately

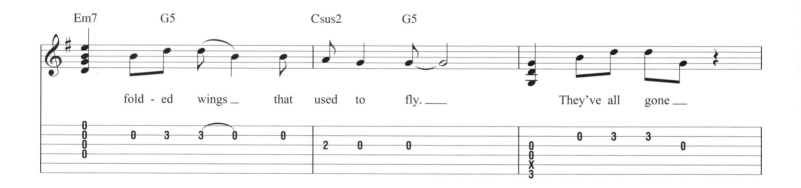

Seen my share of bro - ken ha - los,

*Optional: To match recording, place capo at 1st fret.

fold - ed wings __ that used to fly. __ They've all gone __

2nd time, To Coda 1
3rd time, To Coda 2

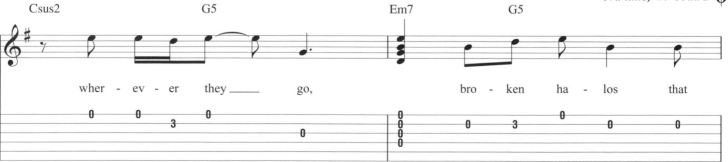

wher - ev - er they __ go, bro - ken ha - los that

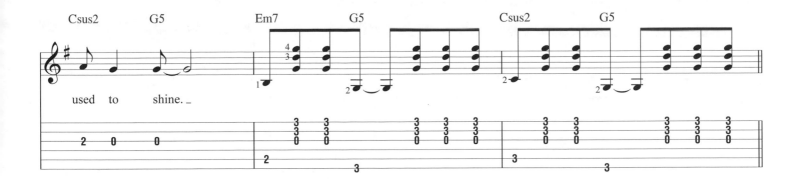

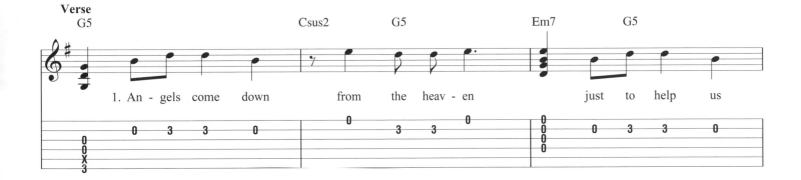

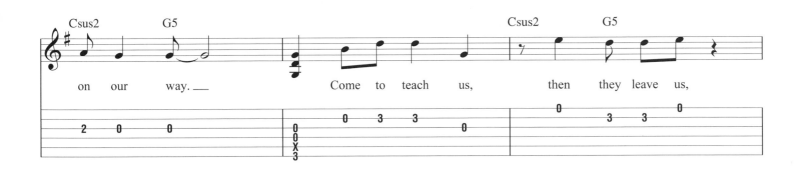

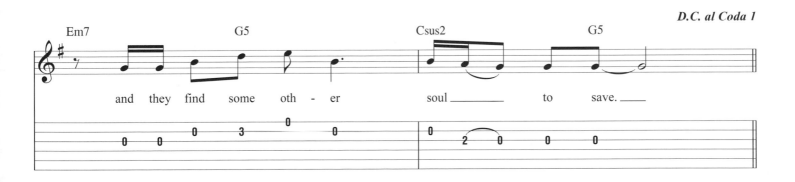

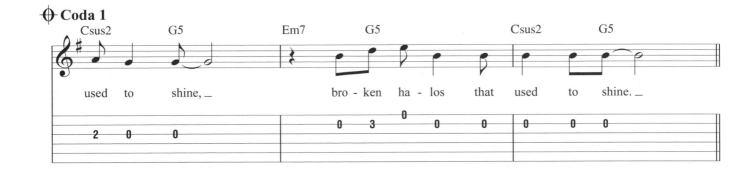

Interlude

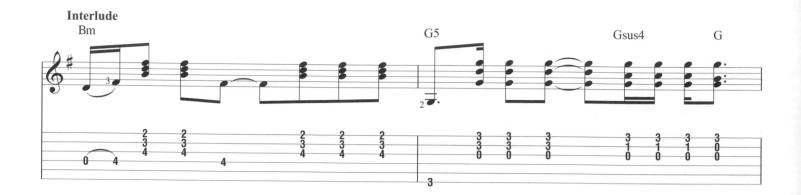

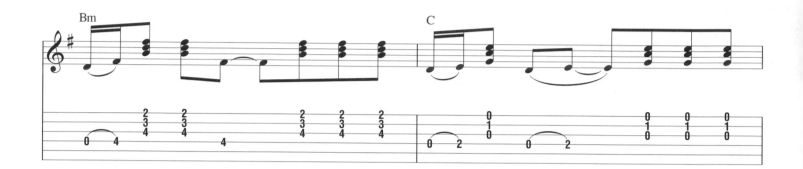

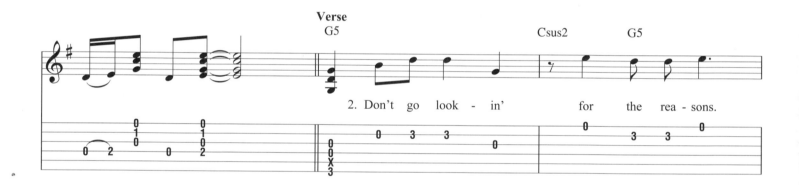

2. Don't go look - in' for the rea - sons.

Don't go ask - in' Je - sus why. ___ We're not meant to

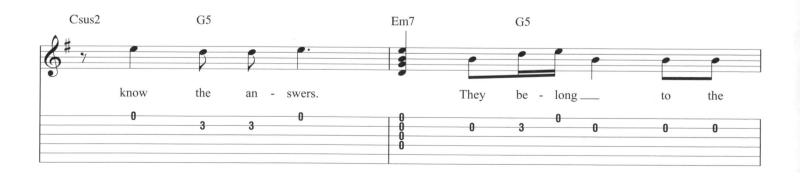

know the an - swers. They be - long ___ to the

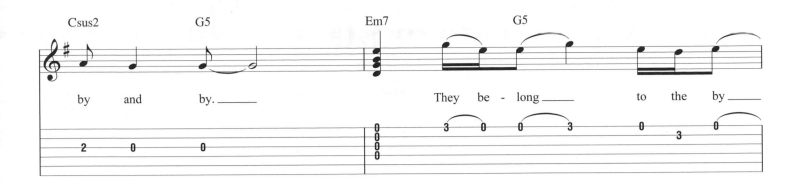

by and by. _____ They be - long _____ to the by _____

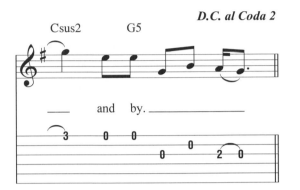

___ and by. _____

D.C. al Coda 2

$\oplus$ **Coda 2**

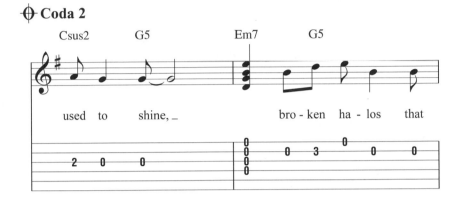

used to shine, _ bro - ken ha - los that

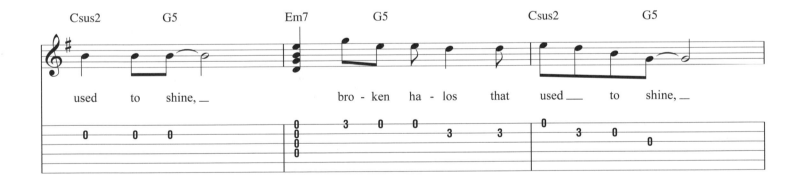

used to shine, _ bro - ken ha - los that used ___ to shine, _

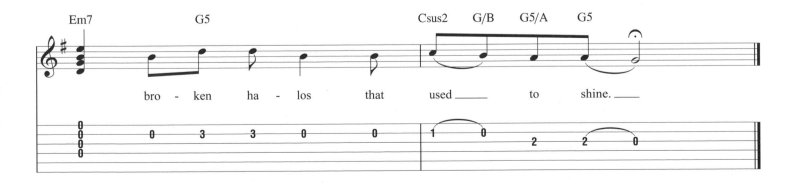

bro - ken ha - los that used _____ to shine. ____

City of Stars

from LA LA LAND

Music by Justin Hurwitz
Lyrics by Benj Pasek & Justin Paul

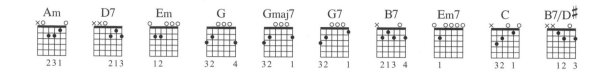

Strum Pattern: 2, 6
Pick Pattern: 2, 5

'cause all that I need's ___ this cra - zy feel - ing, a rat - tat - tat on my heart... ___

Sebastian:
___ Think I want it to stay.

Cit - y of stars, ___ are you shin - ing just for me?

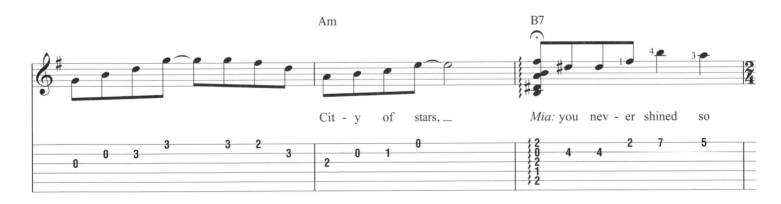

Cit - y of stars, ___ *Mia:* you nev - er shined so

bright - ly. *rit.* Harm.

Despacito

Words and Music by Luis Fonsi, Erika Ender, Justin Bieber, Jason Boyd, Marty James Garton and Ramón Ayala

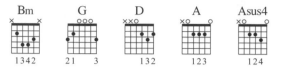

Strum Pattern: 3
Pick Pattern: 3

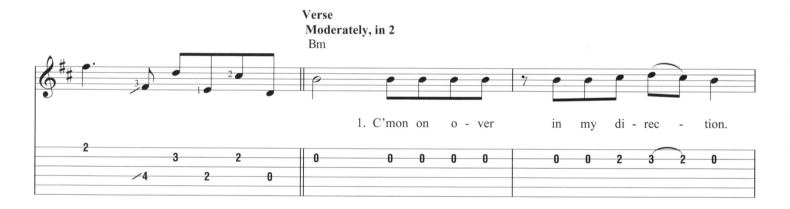

1. C'mon on o - ver in my di - rec - tion.

So thank - ful for that, it's such a bless - in', ___ yeah. Turn ev - 'ry sit - u -

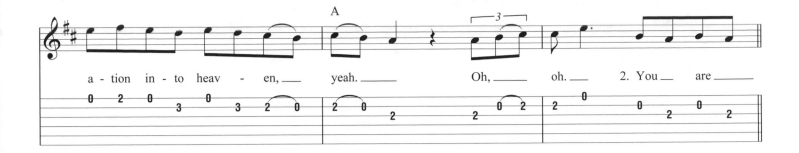

a - tion in - to heav - en, ____ yeah. Oh, ____ oh. ____ 2. You ____ are ____

Verse

____ my sun - rise on the dark - est day. ____ Got me

feel - in' some kind of way. ____ Make me wan - na sa - vor ev - 'ry mo - ment

Verse

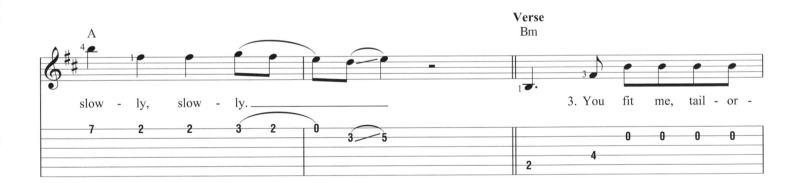

slow - ly, slow - ly. ____ 3. You fit me, tail - or -

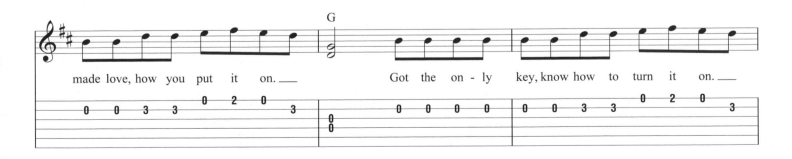

made love, how you put it on. ____ Got the on - ly key, know how to turn it on. ____

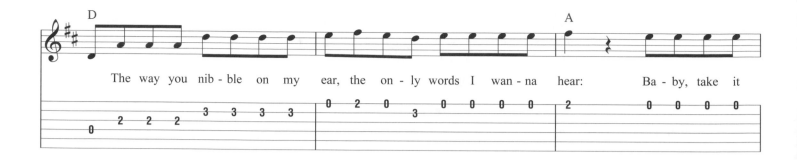

The way you nib - ble on my ear, the on - ly words I wan - na hear: Ba - by, take it

Verse

slow so we can last long. __ 4. Tú, tú e - res el i - mán y yo soy el me -
5. *See additional lyrics*

tal. Me voy a - cer - can - do y voy ar - man - do el plan. Só - lo con pen -

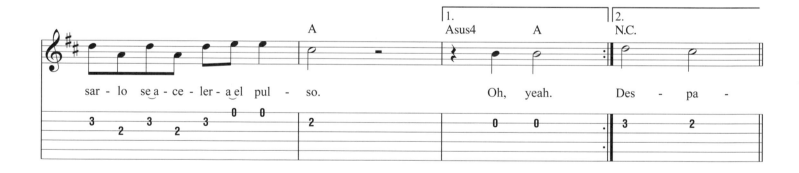

sar - lo se a - ce - ler - a el pul - so. Oh, yeah. Des - pa -

Chorus

ci - to. Quie - ro res - pi - rar tu cue - llo des - pa - ci - to. De - ja que te

di - ga co - sas al o - í - do, pa - ra que te a - cuer - des si no es - tás con mi -

- go. Des - pa - ci - to. Quie - ro des - nu - dar - te a be - sos des - pa - ci -

- to, fir - mo en las pa - re - des de tu la - be - rin - to, y ha - cer de tu

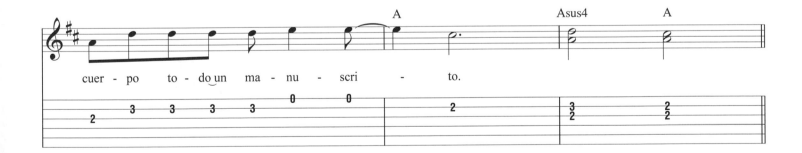

cuer - po to - do un ma - nu - scri - to.

Verse

6., 12. Quie - ro ver bai - lar tu pe - lo, quie - ro ser tu rit - mo,
7., 13. *See additional lyrics*

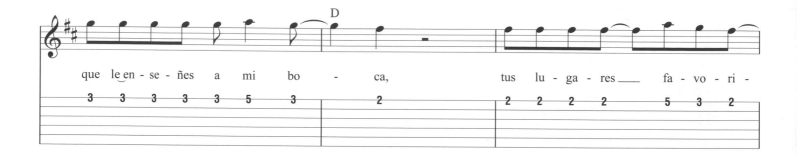

que le en - se - ñes a mi bo - ca, tus lu - ga - res___ fa - vo - ri -

- tos.___   8. Si te pi - do un be - so, ven

Verse

dá - me - lo.___ Yo sé que es - tás pen - sán - do - lo.___ Lle - vo tiem - po in - ten -
9., 10., 11. *See additional lyrics*

tán - do - lo, ___ ma - mi es - to es dan - do y dán - do - lo. ___ Sa - bes que tu cor - a - zón con - mi - go te ha - ce

bang bang. Sa - bes que e - sa be - ba es - tá bus - can - do de mi bang bang. 9. Ven prue - ba de mi

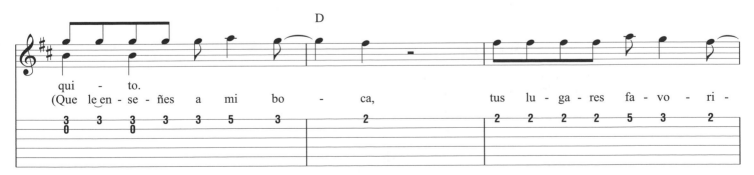

Outro

Pa - si - to_a pa - si - to, sua - ve sua - ve - ci - to. Nos va - mos pe -

- tos.) gan - do, po - qui - to_a po - qui - to.
(Has - ta pro - vo - car tus gri - tos.)

Y que_ol - vi - des tu_a - pe - lli - do. Des - pa - ci - to.

Additional Lyrics

5. Ya, ya me_está gustando más de lo normal.
   Todos mis sentidos vanpidiendo más.
   Esto_hay que tomarlo sin ningún a puro.

7., 13. Déjame sobrepasar tus zonas de peligro,
   Hasta provocar tus gritos,
   Y que_olvides tu_apellido.

9. Ven prueba de mi boca para ver como te sabe.
   Quiero, quiero, quiero ver cuánto amor a ti te cabe.
   Yo no tengo prisa, yo me quiero dar el viaje,
   Empecemos lento, después salvaje.

10. Pasito_a pasito, suave suave cito.
   Nos vamos pegando poquito_a poquito
   Cuando tú me besas con esa de streza,
   Veo que_eres malicia con delicadeza.

11. Pasito_a pasito, suave suavecito.
   No vamos pegando poquito_a poquito.
   Y_es que esa belleza en un rompeca bezas,
   Pero pa'montarlo_aqui tengo la pieza. ¡O ye!

Human

Words and Music by Jamie Hartman and Rory Graham

*Tune down 1/2 step:

(low to high) Eb-Ab-Db-Gb-Bb-Eb

Strum Pattern: 1

Pick Pattern: 1

Intro

Moderately slow, in 2

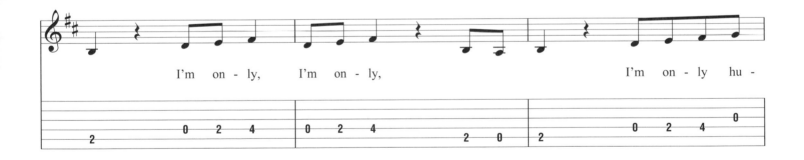

*Optional: To match recording, tune down1/2 step.

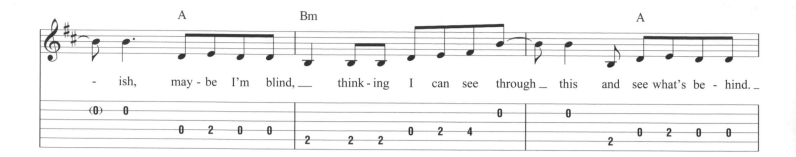

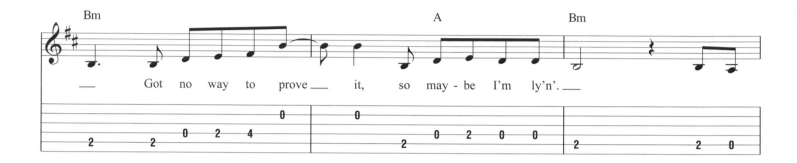

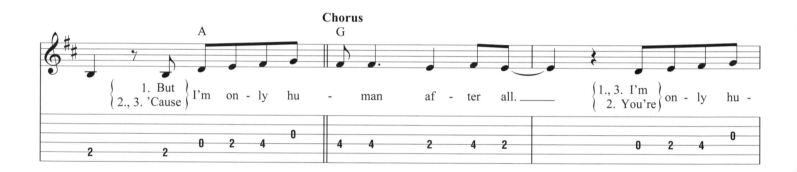

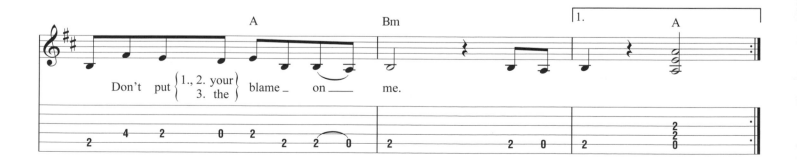

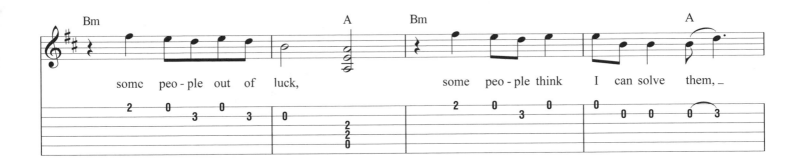

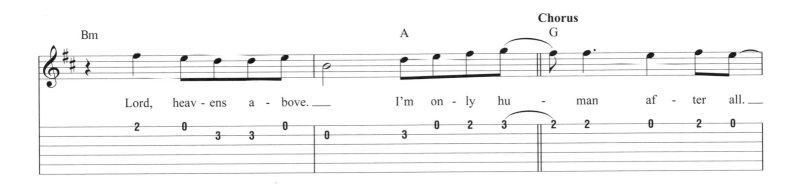

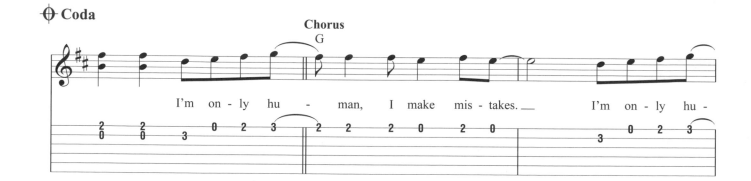

Chorus

I'm on-ly hu-man, I make mis-takes. ___ I'm on-ly hu-

- man, it's all it takes ___ to put the blame ___ on ___ me.

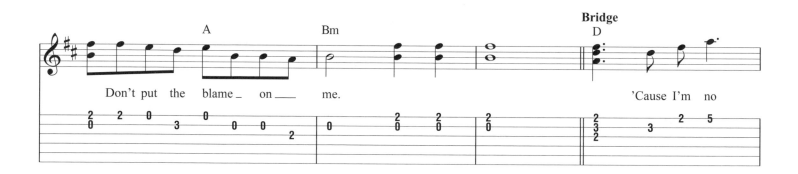

Bridge

Don't put the blame ___ on ___ me. 'Cause I'm no

pro-phet or mes-si - ah, you should go

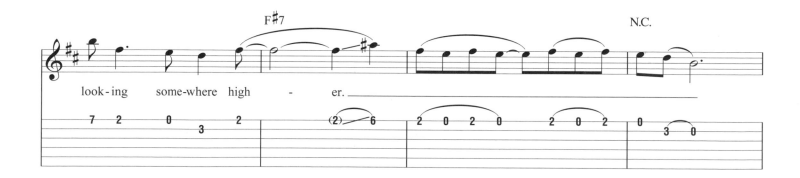

look-ing some-where high - er. ___

I'm on-ly hu - man af - ter all. ___ I'm on-ly hu - man af - ter all. ___

___ Don't put the blame on ___ me. Don't put the blame on ___ me.

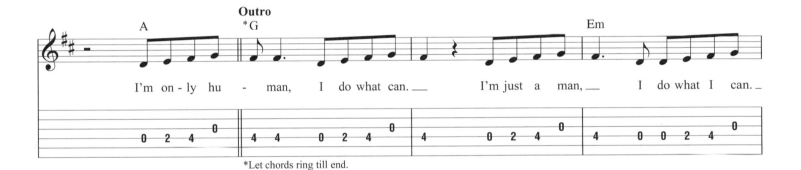

I'm on-ly hu - man, I do what can. ___ I'm just a man, ___ I do what I can. ___

*Let chords ring till end.

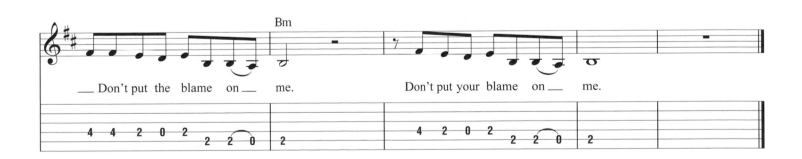

___ Don't put the blame on ___ me. Don't put your blame on ___ me.

Additional Lyrics

2. Take a look in the mirror and what do you see?
   Do you see it clearer or are you deceived
   In what you believed?

3. Don't ask my opinion, don't ask me to lie
   Then beg for forgiveness for making you cry,
   For making you cry.

Look What You Made Me Do

Words and Music by Taylor Swift, Jack Antonoff, Richard Fairbrass, Fred Fairbrass and Rob Manzoli

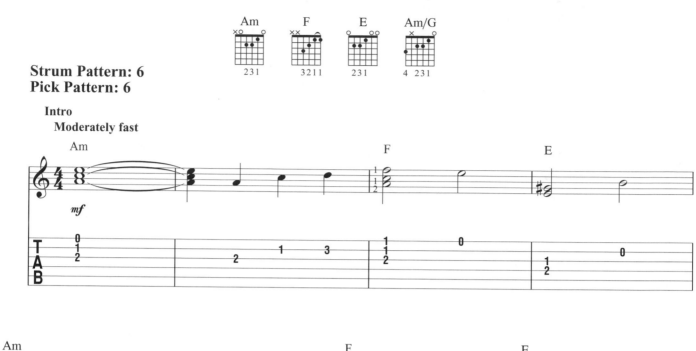

Strum Pattern: 6
Pick Pattern: 6

Intro
Moderately fast

Verse

1. I don't like your lit-tle games, don't like your tilt-ed
3. I don't like your king-dom keys, they, once be-longed to

stage, the role you made me play of the fool, no, I don't like you.
me. You asked me for a place to sleep, locked me out and threw a feast.

Verse

N.C.(Am)

2. I don't like your per - fect crime, how
Rap: 4. *The world moves on an - oth - er day, an - oth - er dra - ma, dra - ma, but not for me, not for me,*

you laugh when you lie. You said the gun was
all I think a - bout is kar - ma. And then the world moves on, but one thing's for sure:

Pre-Chorus

Am

mine. Is - n't cool. No, I don't like you. But I got smart - er, I got
may - be I got mine but you'll all get yours.

Am/G

hard - er in the nick of time. Hon - ey, I rose up from the dead, I do it all the time.

F

E

I've got a list of names and yours is in red, un - der - lined. I check it once, then I

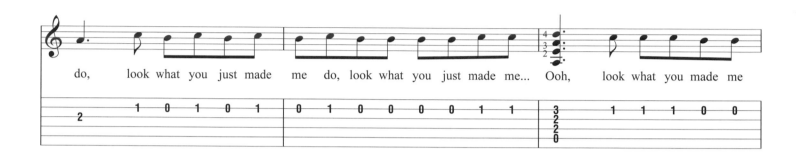

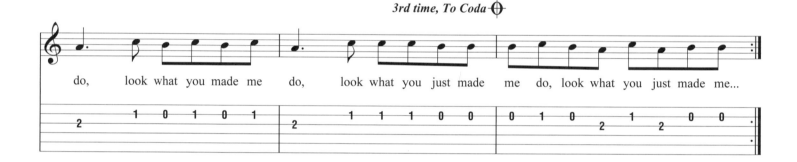

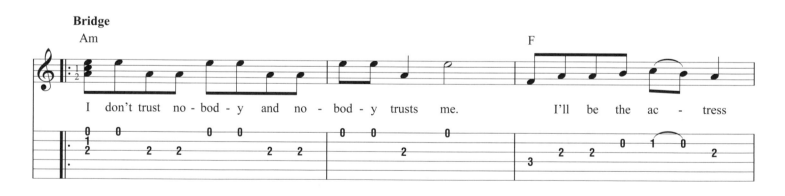

Am/G   F

Spoken: I'm sorry,   *the old Taylor can't come to the phone right now.*

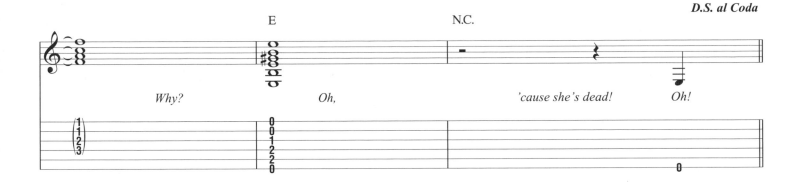

D.S. al Coda

E   N.C.

Why?   *Oh,*   *'cause she's dead!*   *Oh!*

⊕ Coda

Outro-Chorus

Am

me   do, look what you just made me...   Ooh,   look what you made me   do,   look what you made me

Am/G   F

do,   look what you just made   me do, look what you just made me...   Ooh,   look what you made me

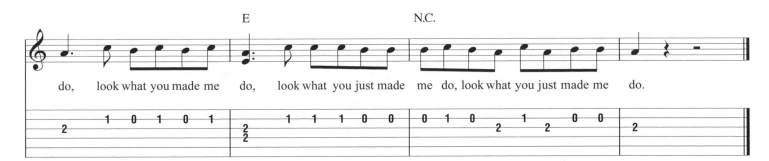

E   N.C.

do,   look what you made me   do,   look what you just made   me do, look what you just made me   do.

Shape of You

Words and Music by Ed Sheeran, Kevin Briggs, Kandi Burruss, Tameka Cottle, Steve Mac and Johnny McDaid

*Capo II

Strum Pattern: 4, 1
Pick Pattern: 6, 4

*Optional: To match recording, place capo at 2nd fret.

**N.C., 2nd time

Pre-Chorus

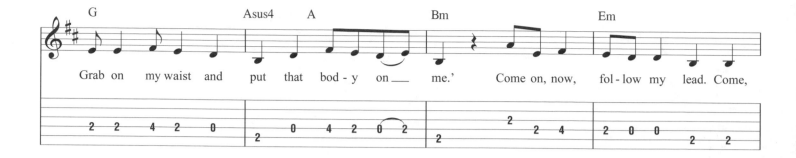

Grab on my waist and put that bod-y on ___ me.' Come on, now, fol-low my lead. Come,

𝄋 Chorus

come on, now, fol-low my lead." Mm. _____ I'm in love with the shape of

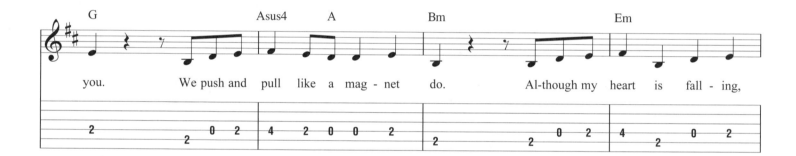

you. We push and pull like a mag-net do. Al-though my heart is fall-ing,

too, I'm in love with your bod - y. Last night you were in my room, and now my

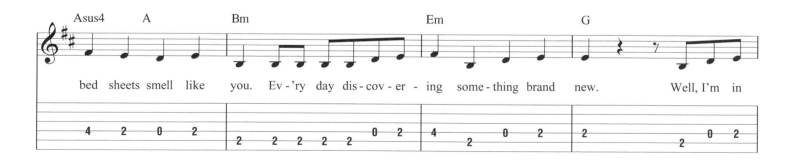

bed sheets smell like you. Ev-'ry day dis-cov-er - ing some-thing brand new. Well, I'm in

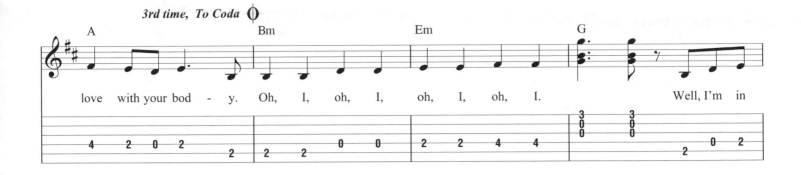

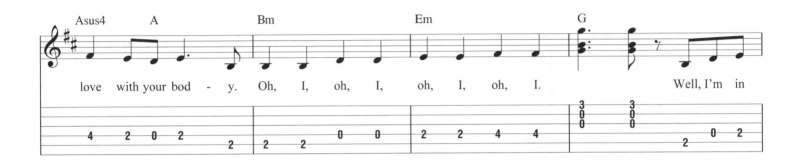

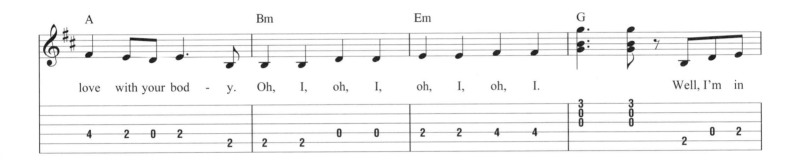

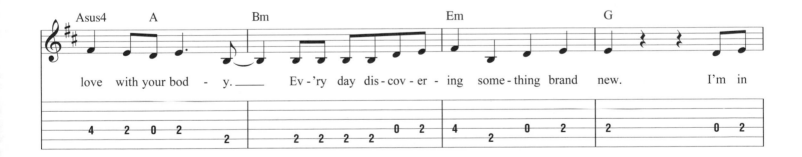

2nd time, D.S. al Coda

Play 3 times

Additional Lyrics

2. One week in, we let the story begin, we're going out on our first date.
You and me are thrifty, so go "all you can eat," fill up your bag and I fill up my plate.
We talk for hours and hours about sweet and the sour, and how your family's doing okay,
And leave and get in a taxi, then kiss in the back seat 'til the driver make the radio play.
And I'm singin' like…

Sign of the Times

Words and Music by Harry Styles, Jeff Bhasker, Alex Salibian, Tyler Johnson, Mitch Rowland and Ryan Nasci

*Capo III

Strum Pattern: 5
Pick Pattern: 5

*Optional: To match recording, place capo at 3rd fret.

1. Just stop your cry - in'; it's the sign of the times.
2. *See additional lyrics*

Wel-come to the fi - nal show. Hope you're wear - in' your best clothes.

You can't bribe the door on your way to the sky.

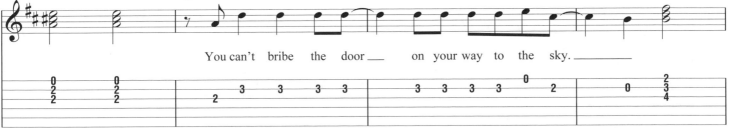

You look pret - ty good _ down here, but you ain't real - ly good. _

% Pre-Chorus

{ 1. They }
{ 2., 3. We } nev - er learn; _ we've been here be - fore. __ Why are we al - ways stuck and

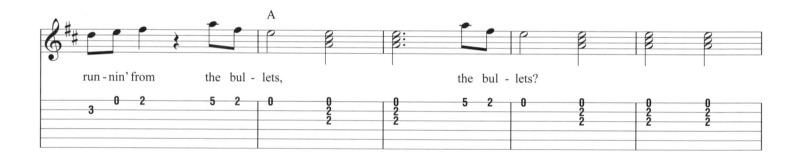

run - nin' from the bul - lets, the bul - lets?

{ They }
{ We } nev - er learn; _ we've been here be - fore. __ Why are we al - ways stuck and

3rd time, To Coda ⊕

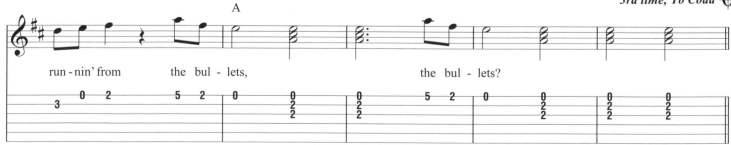

run - nin' from the bul - lets, the bul - lets?

Chorus

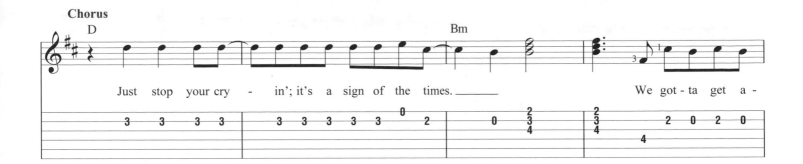

Just stop your cry - in'; it's a sign of the times. _____ We got - ta get a -

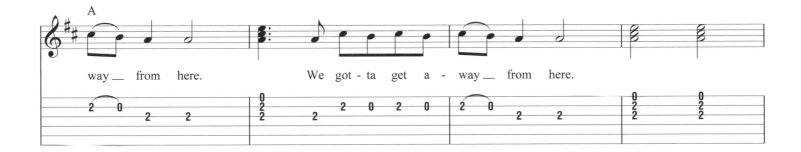

way _ from here. We got - ta get a - way _ from here.

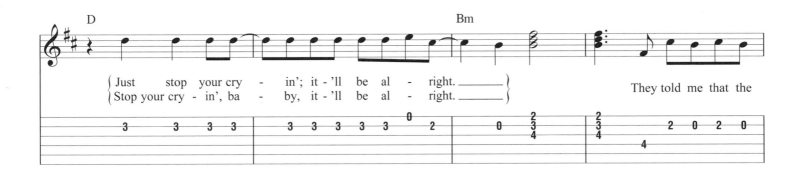

Just stop your cry - in'; it - 'll be al - right. _____
Stop your cry - in', ba - by, it - 'll be al - right. _____

They told me that the

2nd time, D.S. al Coda

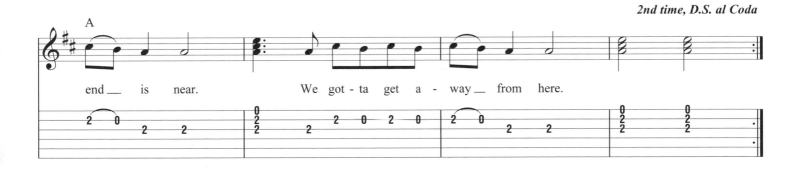

end _ is near. We got - ta get a - way _ from here.

Coda
Bridge

We don't talk e - nough. We should o - pen _ up

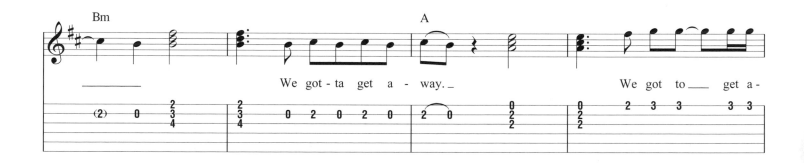

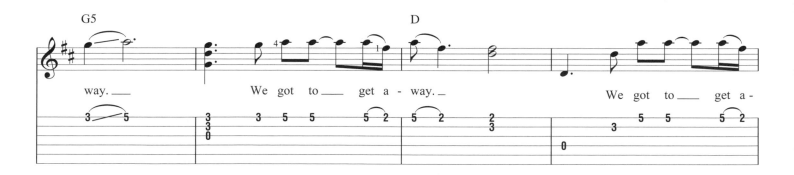

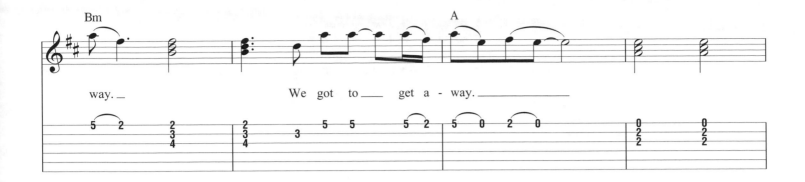

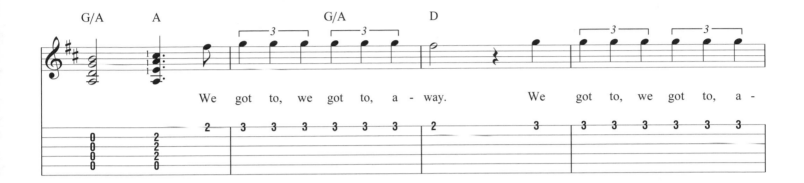

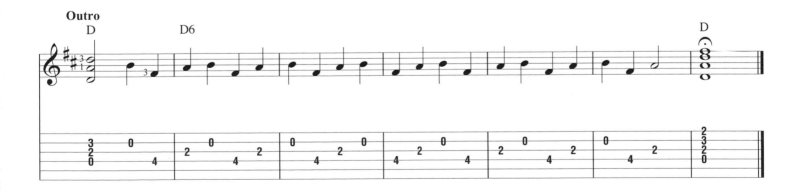

Additional Lyrics

2. Just stop your cryin'; have the time of your life.
Breakin' through the atmosphere, and things are pretty good from here.
Remember, everything will be alright.
We can meet again somewhere, somewhere far away from here.

Slow Hands

Words and Music by Niall Horan, John Henry Ryan, Alexander Izquierdo, Ruth-Anne Cunningham, Tobias Jesso Jr. and Julian Bunetta

Strum Pattern: 1
Pick Pattern: 5

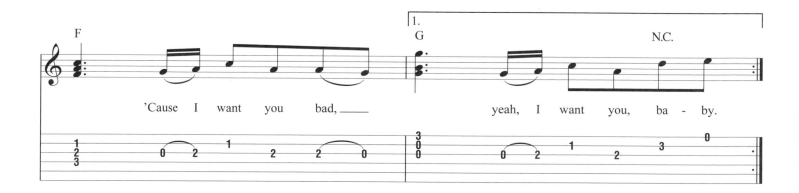

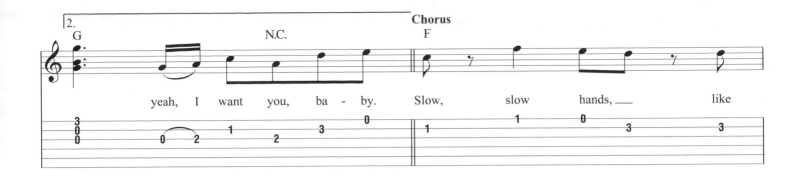

yeah, I want you, ba - by. Slow, slow hands, ___ like

sweat drip - pin' down our dirt - y laun - dry. No, no chance ___ that I'm

leav - in' here with - out you on me. I, I know, ___ yeah, I

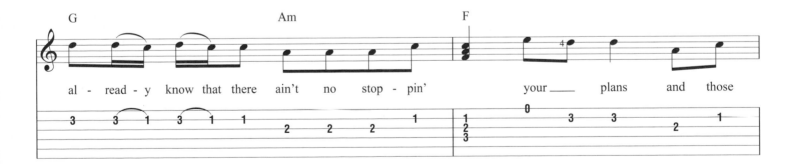

al - read - y know that there ain't no stop - pin' your ___ plans and those

slow ___ hands. (Woo!)   Slow hands.

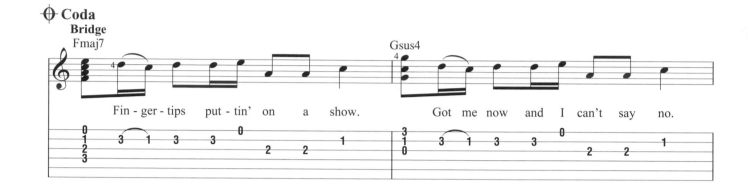

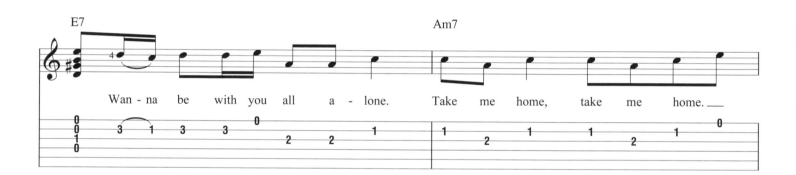

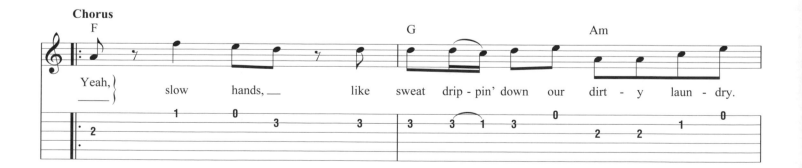

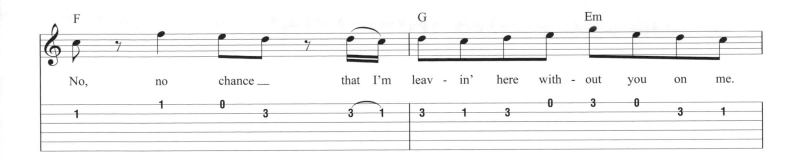

No, no chance ___ that I'm leav-in' here with-out you on me.

I, I know, ___ yeah, I al-read-y know that there ain't no stop-pin...

Outro

Your ___ plans and those slow ___ hands. (Woo!)

Your slow hands. Ooh. Slow hands.

Additional Lyrics

2. I've been thinkin' 'bout it all day.
   And I hope you feel the same way, yeah.
   'Cause I want you bad,
   Yeah, I want you, baby.

3. I just wanna take my time.
   We could do this, baby, all night, yeah.
   'Cause I want you bad,
   Yeah, I want you, baby.

There's Nothing Holdin' Me Back

Words and Music by Shawn Mendes, Geoffrey Warburton, Teddy Geiger and Scott Harris

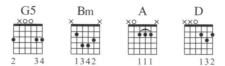

Strum Pattern: 1
Pick Pattern: 2

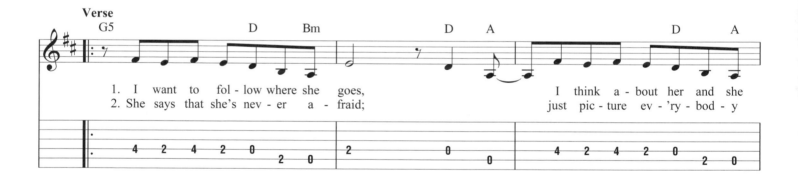

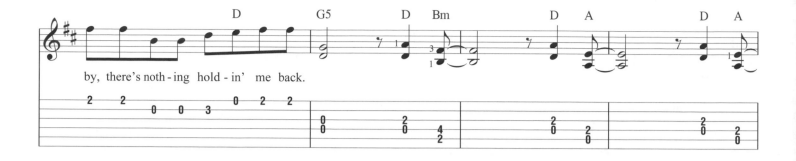

by, there's noth-ing hold-in' me back.

To Coda ⊕

There's noth-ing hold-in' me back.

1. There's noth-ing hold-in' me back.

2. 'Cause if we lost our minds and we took

Bridge

it way too far, I know we'd be al-right, I know we would be al-right. If you were

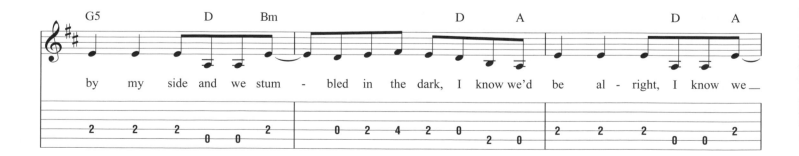

by my side and we stum - bled in the dark, I know we'd be al-right, I know we

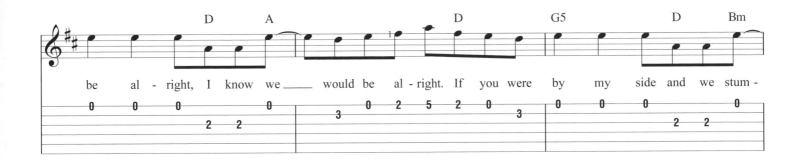

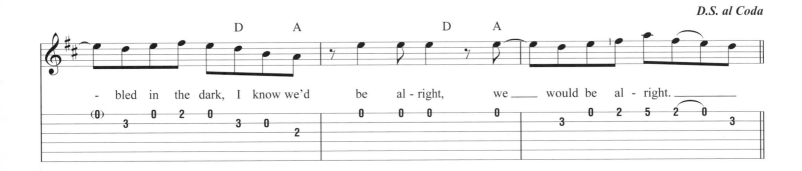

D.S. al Coda

Coda

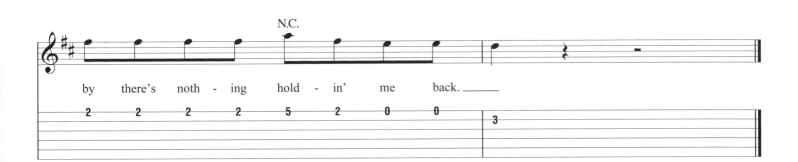

That's What I Like

Words and Music by Bruno Mars, Philip Lawrence, James Fauntleroy, Ray Charles McCullough II,
Christopher Brody Brown, Jeremy Reeves, Jonathan Yip and Ray Romulus

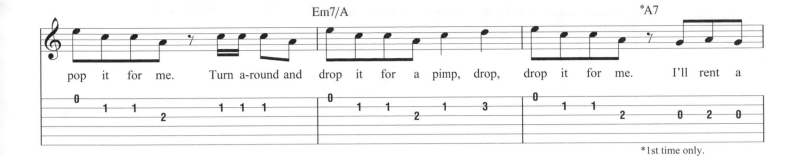

*1st time only.

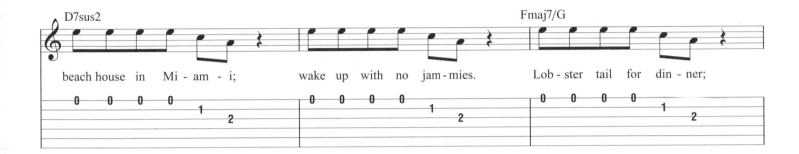

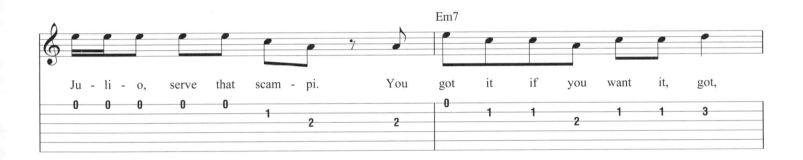

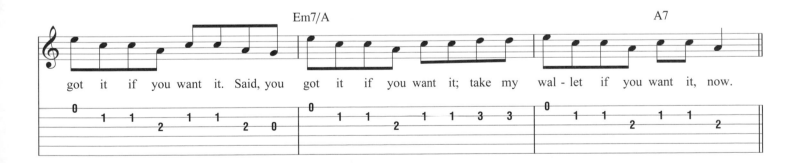

Pre-Chorus

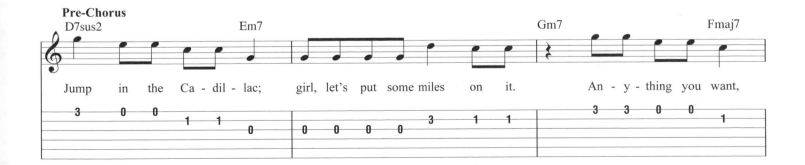

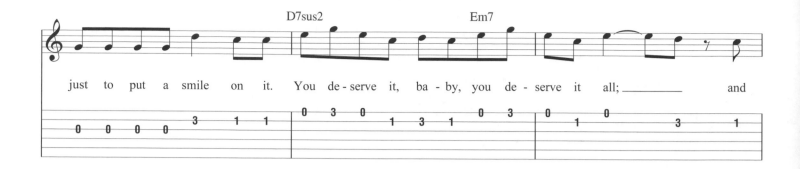

just to put a smile on it. You de - serve it, ba - by, you de - serve it all; _____ and

𝄋 Chorus

I'm gon - na give it to ___ you. Gold jew'l - ry shin - ing so bright; straw - ber - ry

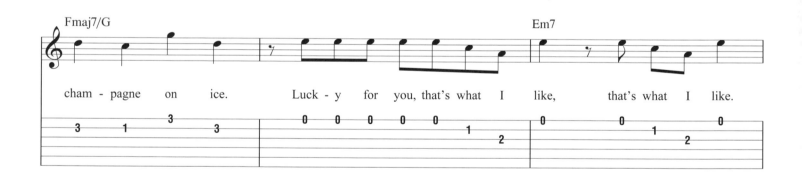

cham - pagne on ice. Luck - y for you, that's what I like, that's what I like.

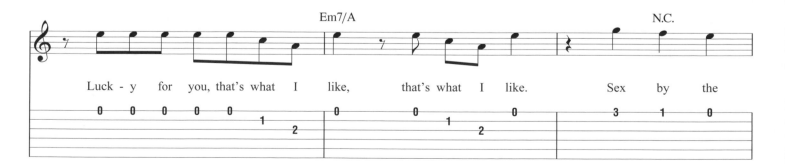

Luck - y for you, that's what I like, that's what I like. Sex by the

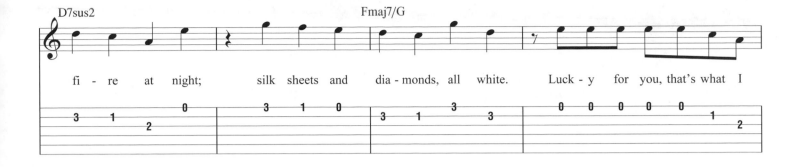

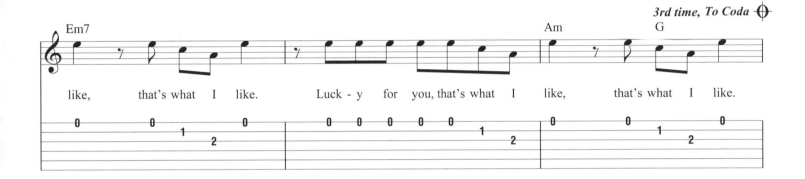

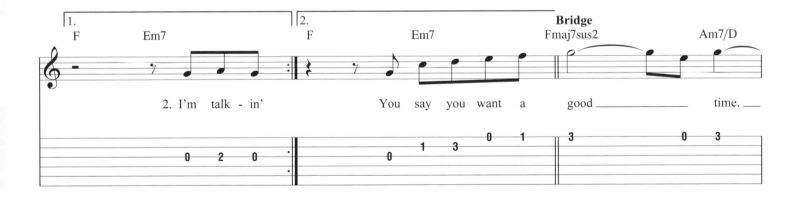

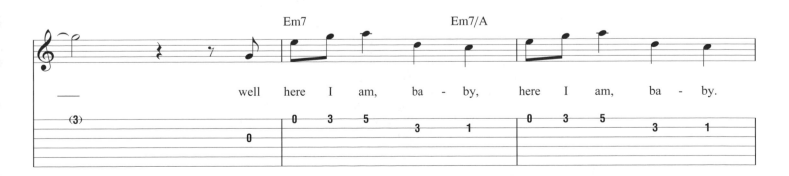

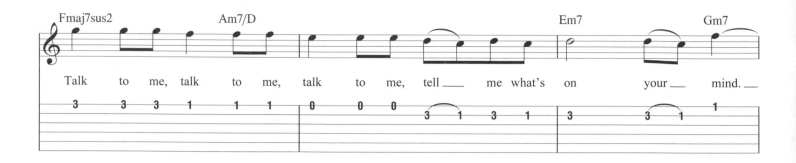

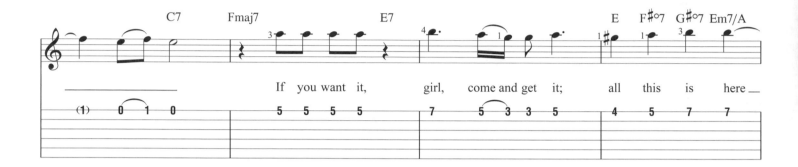

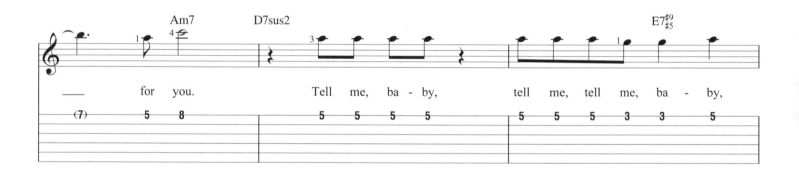

D.S. al Coda

⊕ Coda

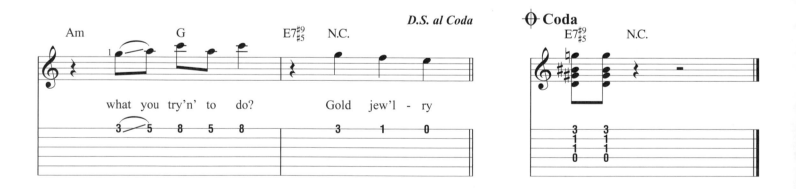

Additional Lyrics

2. I'm talkin' trips to Puerto Rico; say the word and we go.
You can be my freaka; girl, I'll be your fleeko, *mamacita.*
I will never make a promise that I can't keep.
I promise that your smile ain't gon' never leave.
Shopping sprees in Paris; everything twenty-four karat.
Take a look in that mirror; now tell me, who's the fairest?
Is it you? (Is it you?) Is it me? (Is it me?)
Say it's us, (Say it's us.) and I'll agree, baby.

EASY GUITAR WITH NOTES & TAB

This series features simplified arrangements with notes, tab, chord charts, and strum and pick patterns.

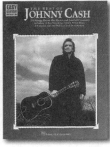

MIXED FOLIOS

00702287	Acoustic	$14.99
00702002	Acoustic Rock Hits for Easy Guitar	$14.99
00702166	All-Time Best Guitar Collection	$19.99
00699665	Beatles Best	$14.99
00702232	Best Acoustic Songs for Easy Guitar	$14.99
00119835	Best Children's Songs	$16.99
00702233	Best Hard Rock Songs	$14.99
00703055	The Big Book of Nursery Rhymes & Children's Songs	$14.99
00322179	The Big Easy Book of Classic Rock Guitar	$24.95
00698978	Big Christmas Collection	$16.95
00702394	Bluegrass Songs for Easy Guitar	$12.99
00703387	Celtic Classics	$14.99
00224808	Chart Hits of 2016-2017	$14.99
00156245	Chart Hits of 2015-2016	$14.99
00702149	Children's Christian Songbook	$9.99
00702237	Christian Acoustic Favorites	$12.95
00702028	Christmas Classics	$8.99
00101779	Christmas Guitar	$14.99
00702185	Christmas Hits	$9.95
00702141	Classic Rock	$8.95
00702203	CMT's 100 Greatest Country Songs	$27.95
00702283	The Contemporary Christian Collection	$16.99

00702239	Country Classics for Easy Guitar	$19.99
00702282	Country Hits of 2009–2010	$14.99
00702257	Easy Acoustic Guitar Songs	$14.99
00702280	Easy Guitar Tab White Pages	$29.99
00702041	Favorite Hymns for Easy Guitar	$10.99
00140841	4-Chord Hymns for Guitar	$7.99
00702281	4 Chord Rock	$10.99
00126894	Frozen	$14.99
00702286	Glee	$16.99
00699374	Gospel Favorites	$14.95
00122138	The Grammy Awards® Record of the Year 1958-2011	$19.99
00702160	The Great American Country Songbook	$16.99
00702050	Great Classical Themes for Easy Guitar	$8.99
00702116	Greatest Hymns for Guitar	$10.99
00702130	The Groovy Years	$9.95
00702184	Guitar Instrumentals	$9.95
00148030	Halloween Guitar Songs	$14.99
00702273	Irish Songs	$12.99
00702275	Jazz Favorites for Easy Guitar	$15.99
00702274	Jazz Standards for Easy Guitar	$15.99
00702162	Jumbo Easy Guitar Songbook	$19.99
00702258	Legends of Rock	$14.99
00702261	Modern Worship Hits	$14.99

00702189	MTV's 100 Greatest Pop Songs	$24.95
00702272	1950s Rock	$15.99
00702271	1960s Rock	$15.99
00702270	1970s Rock	$15.99
00702269	1980s Rock	$14.99
00702268	1990s Rock	$14.99
00109725	Once	$14.99
00702187	Selections from O Brother Where Art Thou?	$14.99
00702178	100 Songs for Kids	$14.99
00702515	Pirates of the Caribbean	$12.99
00702125	Praise and Worship for Guitar	$10.99
00702285	Southern Rock Hits	$12.99
00121535	30 Easy Celtic Guitar Solos	$14.99
00702220	Today's Country Hits	$9.95
00121900	Today's Women of Pop & Rock	$14.99
00702294	Top Worship Hits	$15.99
00702255	VH1's 100 Greatest Hard Rock Songs	$27.99
00702175	VH1's 100 Greatest Songs of Rock and Roll	$24.95
00702253	Wicked	$12.99

ARTIST COLLECTIONS

00702267	AC/DC for Easy Guitar	$15.99
00702598	Adele for Easy Guitar	$15.99
00702040	Best of the Allman Brothers	$14.99
00702865	J.S. Bach for Easy Guitar	$14.99
00702169	Best of The Beach Boys	$12.99
00702292	The Beatles — 1	$19.99
00125796	Best of Chuck Berry	$14.99
00702201	The Essential Black Sabbath	$12.95
02501615	Zac Brown Band — The Foundation	$16.99
02501621	Zac Brown Band — You Get What You Give	$16.99
00702043	Best of Johnny Cash	$16.99
00702263	Best of Casting Crowns	$14.99
00702090	Eric Clapton's Best	$10.95
00702086	Eric Clapton — from the Album Unplugged	$10.95
00702202	The Essential Eric Clapton	$14.99
00702250	blink-182 — Greatest Hits	$15.99
00702053	Best of Patsy Cline	$12.99
00702229	The Very Best of Creedence Clearwater Revival	$15.99
00702145	Best of Jim Croce	$15.99
00702278	Crosby, Stills & Nash	$12.99
00702219	David Crowder*Band Collection	$12.95
14042809	Bob Dylan	$14.99
00702276	Fleetwood Mac — Easy Guitar Collection	$14.99
00130952	Foo Fighters	$14.99
00139462	The Very Best of Grateful Dead	$14.99
00702136	Best of Merle Haggard	$12.99
00702227	Jimi Hendrix — Smash Hits	$14.99
00702288	Best of Hillsong United	$12.99
00702236	Best of Antonio Carlos Jobim	$12.95

00702245	Elton John — Greatest Hits 1970–2002	$14.99
00129855	Jack Johnson	$14.99
00702204	Robert Johnson	$10.99
00702234	Selections from Toby Keith — 35 Biggest Hits	$12.95
00702003	Kiss	$10.99
00110578	Best of Kutless	$12.99
00702216	Lynyrd Skynyrd	$15.99
00702182	The Essential Bob Marley	$12.95
00146081	Maroon 5	$14.99
00121925	Bruno Mars – Unorthodox Jukebox	$12.99
00702248	Paul McCartney — All the Best	$14.99
00702129	Songs of Sarah McLachlan	$12.95
00125484	The Best of MercyMe	$12.99
02501316	Metallica — Death Magnetic	$17.99
00702209	Steve Miller Band — Young Hearts (Greatest Hits)	$12.95
00124167	Jason Mraz	$14.99
00702096	Best of Nirvana	$15.99
00702211	The Offspring — Greatest Hits	$12.95
00138026	One Direction	$14.99
00702030	Best of Roy Orbison	$12.95
00702144	Best of Ozzy Osbourne	$14.99
00702279	Tom Petty	$12.99
00102911	Pink Floyd	$16.99
00702139	Elvis Country Favorites	$12.99
00702293	The Very Best of Prince	$14.99
00699415	Best of Queen for Guitar	$14.99
00109279	Best of R.E.M.	$14.99
00702208	Red Hot Chili Peppers — Greatest Hits	$12.95

00174793	The Very Best of Santana	$14.99
00702196	Best of Bob Seger	$12.95
00146046	Ed Sheeran	$14.99
00702252	Frank Sinatra — Nothing But the Best	$12.99
00702010	Best of Rod Stewart	$16.99
00702049	Best of George Strait	$14.99
00702259	Taylor Swift for Easy Guitar	$15.99
00702260	Taylor Swift — Fearless	$14.99
00139727	Taylor Swift — 1989	$17.99
00115960	Taylor Swift — Red	$16.99
00702290	Taylor Swift — Speak Now	$15.99
00702226	Chris Tomlin — See the Morning	$12.95
00148643	Train	$14.99
00702427	U2 — 18 Singles	$14.99
00102711	Van Halen	$16.99
00702108	Best of Stevie Ray Vaughan	$14.99
00702123	Best of Hank Williams	$14.99
00702111	Stevie Wonder — Guitar Collection	$9.95
00702228	Neil Young — Greatest Hits	$15.99
00119133	Neil Young — Harvest	$14.99
00702188	Essential ZZ Top	$10.95

HAL•LEONARD®

Visit Hal Leonard online at
www.halleonard.com

0917

HAL•LEONARD® GUITAR PLAY-ALONG

AUDIO ACCESS INCLUDED

This series will help you play your favorite songs quickly and easily. Just follow the tab and listen to the audio to the hear how the guitar should sound, and then play along using the separate backing tracks. Audio files also include software to slow down the tempo without changing pitch. The melody and lyrics are included in the book so that you can sing or simply follow along.

INCLUDES TAB

VOL. 1 – ROCK	00699570 / $16.99	
VOL. 2 – ACOUSTIC	00699569 / $16.99	
VOL. 3 – HARD ROCK	00699573 / $17.99	
VOL. 4 – POP/ROCK	00699571 / $16.99	
VOL. 6 – '90S ROCK	00699572 / $16.99	
VOL. 7 – BLUES	00699575 / $17.99	
VOL. 8 – ROCK	00699585 / $16.99	
VOL. 9 – EASY ACOUSTIC SONGS	00151708 / $16.99	
VOL. 10 – ACOUSTIC	00699586 / $16.95	
VOL. 11 – EARLY ROCK	00699579 / $14.95	
VOL. 12 – POP/ROCK	00699587 / $14.95	
VOL. 13 – FOLK ROCK	00699581 / $15.99	
VOL. 14 – BLUES ROCK	00699582 / $16.99	
VOL. 15 – R&B	00699583 / $16.99	
VOL. 16 – JAZZ	00699584 / $15.95	
VOL. 17 – COUNTRY	00699588 / $16.99	
VOL. 18 – ACOUSTIC ROCK	00699577 / $15.95	
VOL. 19 – SOUL	00699578 / $15.99	
VOL. 20 – ROCKABILLY	00699580 / $14.95	
VOL. 21 – SANTANA	00174525 / $17.99	
VOL. 22 – CHRISTMAS	00699600 / $15.99	
VOL. 23 – SURF	00699635 / $15.99	
VOL. 24 – ERIC CLAPTON	00699649 / $17.99	
VOL. 25 – THE BEATLES	00198265 / $17.99	
VOL. 26 – ELVIS PRESLEY	00699643 / $16.99	
VOL. 27 – DAVID LEE ROTH	00699645 / $16.95	
VOL. 28 – GREG KOCH	00699646 / $16.99	
VOL. 29 – BOB SEGER	00699647 / $15.99	
VOL. 30 – KISS	00699644 / $16.99	
VOL. 31 – CHRISTMAS HITS	00699652 / $14.95	
VOL. 32 – THE OFFSPRING	00699653 / $14.95	
VOL. 33 – ACOUSTIC CLASSICS	00699656 / $17.99	
VOL. 34 – CLASSIC ROCK	00699658 / $17.99	
VOL. 35 – HAIR METAL	00699660 / $17.99	
VOL. 36 – SOUTHERN ROCK	00699661 / $16.95	
VOL. 37 – ACOUSTIC UNPLUGGED	00699662 / $22.99	
VOL. 38 – BLUES	00699663 / $16.95	
VOL. 39 – '80S METAL	00699664 / $16.99	
VOL. 40 – INCUBUS	00699668 / $17.95	
VOL. 41 – ERIC CLAPTON	00699669 / $17.99	
VOL. 42 – COVER BAND HITS	00211597 / $16.99	
VOL. 43 – LYNYRD SKYNYRD	00699681 / $17.95	
VOL. 44 – JAZZ	00699689 / $16.99	
VOL. 45 – TV THEMES	00699718 / $14.95	
VOL. 46 – MAINSTREAM ROCK	00699722 / $16.95	
VOL. 47 – HENDRIX SMASH HITS	00699723 / $19.99	
VOL. 48 – AEROSMITH CLASSICS	00699724 / $17.99	
VOL. 49 – STEVIE RAY VAUGHAN	00699725 / $17.99	
VOL. 50 – VAN HALEN 1978-1984	00110269 / $17.99	
VOL. 51 – ALTERNATIVE '90S	00699727 / $14.99	
VOL. 52 – FUNK	00699728 / $15.99	
VOL. 53 – DISCO	00699729 / $14.99	
VOL. 54 – HEAVY METAL	00699730 / $15.99	
VOL. 55 – POP METAL	00699731 / $14.95	
VOL. 56 – FOO FIGHTERS	00699749 / $15.99	
VOL. 59 – CHET ATKINS	00702347 / $16.99	
VOL. 62 – CHRISTMAS CAROLS	00699798 / $12.95	
VOL. 63 – CREEDENCE CLEARWATER REVIVAL	00699802 / $16.99	
VOL. 64 – THE ULTIMATE OZZY OSBOURNE	00699803 / $17.99	
VOL. 66 – THE ROLLING STONES	00699807 / $17.99	
VOL. 67 – BLACK SABBATH	00699808 / $16.99	

VOL. 68 – PINK FLOYD – DARK SIDE OF THE MOON	00699809 / $16.99	
VOL. 69 – ACOUSTIC FAVORITES	00699810 / $16.99	
VOL. 70 – OZZY OSBOURNE	00699805 / $16.99	
VOL. 71 – CHRISTIAN ROCK	00699824 / $14.95	
VOL. 73 – BLUESY ROCK	00699829 / $16.99	
VOL. 74 – SIMPLE STRUMMING SONGS	00151706 / $19.99	
VOL. 75 – TOM PETTY	00699882 / $16.99	
VOL. 76 – COUNTRY HITS	00699884 / $14.95	
VOL. 77 – BLUEGRASS	00699910 / $15.99	
VOL. 78 – NIRVANA	00700132 / $16.99	
VOL. 79 – NEIL YOUNG	00700133 / $24.99	
VOL. 80 – ACOUSTIC ANTHOLOGY	00700175 / $19.95	
VOL. 81 – ROCK ANTHOLOGY	00700176 / $22.99	
VOL. 82 – EASY SONGS	00700177 / $14.99	
VOL. 83 – THREE CHORD SONGS	00700178 / $16.99	
VOL. 84 – STEELY DAN	00700200 / $16.99	
VOL. 85 – THE POLICE	00700269 / $16.99	
VOL. 86 – BOSTON	00700465 / $16.99	
VOL. 87 – ACOUSTIC WOMEN	00700763 / $14.99	
VOL. 89 – REGGAE	00700468 / $15.99	
VOL. 90 – CLASSICAL POP	00700469 / $14.99	
VOL. 91 – BLUES INSTRUMENTALS	00700505 / $15.99	
VOL. 92 – EARLY ROCK INSTRUMENTALS	00700506 / $15.99	
VOL. 93 – ROCK INSTRUMENTALS	00700507 / $16.99	
VOL. 94 – SLOW BLUES	00700508 / $16.99	
VOL. 95 – BLUES CLASSICS	00700509 / $14.99	
VOL. 99 – ZZ TOP	00700762 / $16.99	
VOL. 100 – B.B. KING	00700466 / $16.99	
VOL. 101 – SONGS FOR BEGINNERS	00701917 / $14.99	
VOL. 102 – CLASSIC PUNK	00700769 / $14.99	
VOL. 103 – SWITCHFOOT	00700773 / $16.99	
VOL. 104 – DUANE ALLMAN	00700846 / $16.99	
VOL. 105 – LATIN	00700939 / $16.99	
VOL. 106 – WEEZER	00700958 / $14.99	
VOL. 107 – CREAM	00701069 / $16.99	
VOL. 108 – THE WHO	00701053 / $16.99	
VOL. 109 – STEVE MILLER	00701054 / $16.99	
VOL. 110 – SLIDE GUITAR HITS	00701055 / $16.99	
VOL. 111 – JOHN MELLENCAMP	00701056 / $14.99	
VOL. 112 – QUEEN	00701052 / $16.99	
VOL. 113 – JIM CROCE	00701058 / $15.99	
VOL. 114 – BON JOVI	00701060 / $16.99	
VOL. 115 – JOHNNY CASH	00701070 / $16.99	
VOL. 116 – THE VENTURES	00701124 / $16.99	
VOL. 117 – BRAD PAISLEY	00701224 / $16.99	
VOL. 118 – ERIC JOHNSON	00701353 / $16.99	
VOL. 119 – AC/DC CLASSICS	00701356 / $17.99	
VOL. 120 – PROGRESSIVE ROCK	00701457 / $14.99	
VOL. 121 – U2	00701508 / $16.99	
VOL. 122 – CROSBY, STILLS & NASH	00701610 / $16.99	
VOL. 123 – LENNON & MCCARTNEY ACOUSTIC	00701614 / $16.99	
VOL. 125 – JEFF BECK	00701687 / $16.99	
VOL. 126 – BOB MARLEY	00701701 / $16.99	
VOL. 127 – 1970S ROCK	00701739 / $16.99	
VOL. 128 – 1960S ROCK	00701740 / $14.99	
VOL. 129 – MEGADETH	00701741 / $16.99	
VOL. 130 – IRON MAIDEN	00701742 / $17.99	
VOL. 131 – 1990S ROCK	00701743 / $14.99	
VOL. 132 – COUNTRY ROCK	00701757 / $15.99	
VOL. 133 – TAYLOR SWIFT	00701894 / $16.99	
VOL. 134 – AVENGED SEVENFOLD	00701906 / $16.99	
VOL. 135 – MINOR BLUES	00151350 / $17.99	

VOL. 136 – GUITAR THEMES	00701922 / $14.99	
VOL. 137 – IRISH TUNES	00701966 / $15.99	
VOL. 138 – BLUEGRASS CLASSICS	00701967 / $14.99	
VOL. 139 – GARY MOORE	00702370 / $16.99	
VOL. 140 – MORE STEVIE RAY VAUGHAN	00702396 / $17.99	
VOL. 141 – ACOUSTIC HITS	00702401 / $16.99	
VOL. 143 – SLASH	00702425 / $19.99	
VOL. 144 – DJANGO REINHARDT	00702531 / $16.99	
VOL. 145 – DEF LEPPARD	00702532 / $17.99	
VOL. 146 – ROBERT JOHNSON	00702533 / $16.99	
VOL. 147 – SIMON & GARFUNKEL	14041591 / $16.99	
VOL. 148 – BOB DYLAN	14041592 / $16.99	
VOL. 149 – AC/DC HITS	14041593 / $17.99	
VOL. 150 – ZAKK WYLDE	02501717 / $16.99	
VOL. 151 – J.S. BACH	02501730 / $16.99	
VOL. 152 – JOE BONAMASSA	02501751 / $19.99	
VOL. 153 – RED HOT CHILI PEPPERS	00702990 / $19.99	
VOL. 155 – ERIC CLAPTON – FROM THE ALBUM UNPLUGGED	00703085 / $16.99	
VOL. 156 – SLAYER	00703770 / $17.99	
VOL. 157 – FLEETWOOD MAC	00101382 / $16.99	
VOL. 158 – ULTIMATE CHRISTMAS	00101889 / $14.99	
VOL. 159 – WES MONTGOMERY	00102593 / $19.99	
VOL. 160 – T-BONE WALKER	00102641 / $16.99	
VOL. 161 – THE EAGLES – ACOUSTIC	00102659 / $17.99	
VOL. 162 – THE EAGLES HITS	00102667 / $17.99	
VOL. 163 – PANTERA	00103036 / $17.99	
VOL. 164 – VAN HALEN 1986-1995	00110270 / $17.99	
VOL. 165 – GREEN DAY	00210343 / $17.99	
VOL. 166 – MODERN BLUES	00700764 / $16.99	
VOL. 167 – DREAM THEATER	00111938 / $24.99	
VOL. 168 – KISS	00113421 / $16.99	
VOL. 169 – TAYLOR SWIFT	00115982 / $16.99	
VOL. 170 – THREE DAYS GRACE	00117337 / $16.99	
VOL. 171 – JAMES BROWN	00117420 / $16.99	
VOL. 172 – THE DOOBIE BROTHERS	00119670 / $16.99	
VOL. 174 – SCORPIONS	00122119 / $16.99	
VOL. 175 – MICHAEL SCHENKER	00122127 / $16.99	
VOL. 176 – BLUES BREAKERS WITH JOHN MAYALL & ERIC CLAPTON	00122132 / $19.99	
VOL. 177 – ALBERT KING	00123271 / $16.99	
VOL. 178 – JASON MRAZ	00124165 / $17.99	
VOL. 179 – RAMONES	00127073 / $16.99	
VOL. 180 – BRUNO MARS	00129706 / $16.99	
VOL. 181 – JACK JOHNSON	00129854 / $16.99	
VOL. 182 – SOUNDGARDEN	00138161 / $17.99	
VOL. 183 – BUDDY GUY	00138240 / $17.99	
VOL. 184 – KENNY WAYNE SHEPHERD	00138258 / $17.99	
VOL. 185 – JOE SATRIANI	00139457 / $17.99	
VOL. 186 – GRATEFUL DEAD	00139459 / $17.99	
VOL. 187 – JOHN DENVER	00140839 / $17.99	
VOL. 188 – MÖTLEY CRUE	00141145 / $17.99	
VOL. 189 – JOHN MAYER	00144350 / $17.99	
VOL. 191 – PINK FLOYD CLASSICS	00146164 / $17.99	
VOL. 192 – JUDAS PRIEST	00151352 / $17.99	

Prices, contents, and availability subject to change without notice.

Complete song lists available online.

HAL•LEONARD®
www.halleonard.com

0817